I AM REVOLUTION

THE BEST LINES

NIRAJ G

Made with ♥ on the Notion Press Platform
www.notionpress.com

Contents

Contents

Contents

Contents

Preface

In the days and the nights,
The Smiles and the fights,
I want to speak out those feelings,
Lay out every emotion, them peelings,
And make them forever mine,
And, luckily enough, I find my pen beside.

1. Twenty-Four hours

No one can be richer than Twenty-four hours,
Toil every day and you won't have more,
You will fatigue and you will fall,
You can Cheque and you can Change,
But a Day is all You will ever have.

2. Fire

Keep your fire burning,

Dark, And Cold, if it burns out.

3. Magic

The Magic of the Night!
Puts the tired to rest,
Gifts sight to see,
Lost Hope blooms to Dream,
Bumbling heart gets the Calm,
And the Wanderer becomes still.

4. Love You

Let me love you,
Night after night,
Today and Tomorrow,
And Again,
I will not keep count,
Let me just go on.

5. Heavens Away

You may be Heavens away,
But I see you,
Every day, Every night,
Up, up in the Open sky,
And I know, you will wait for me, till my Bye.

6. The Book

I read a Book, A Monsoon and Thirteen pages long, Well bound,
A Poetical Gem of Bored sitting and Forced sleeping!
Unfolding layers of The Sky in the Wrath and Rain of days,
Telling the Story of Routine and Chaos of time,
Of each and every person living and dying, Healthy and Un!
Author fails to mention name, to, in, Every Man.

7. Rainbow

The Rainbow is a sign of God existing in monsoon.

8. Man in the Mirror

The Man in the Mirror,
Does exactly that I do,
Smile, Cry, when I do,
Breathes my Air,
Times I think he was born the Day I was,
By my side,

Fool, He knows not,
Can He ever be Me, No!
He will always be on The Other Side.

9. Bedded

Don't lie,
I know the night is important to you,
So I can keep you awake.

10. Don't Hide

The Soul you hide finds Love in the Darkest hours of life,
And that is the moment, Your moment,
When the thundering black clouds that once were,
Will open up the Sky for you to Fly.

11. Sweet Home

If you don't have a place to sleep,
You can ask me,
I can't give you one,
I can only tell how it feels.

12. Explosive

I heard noisy prating, bang-bang hitting,
I came out to silent singing, ting-a-ling jingling,
I walked straight, eddies circling,
I laid down, hopping-lee-bouncing,
Before I go crazy, Fly me in a Box, Sleep slumbering.

13. Wiser with The Book

Man is wiser than the book,
I don't read,
And I don't agree.

14. You and Me

Dreamless nights are better for me,
Even in dreams, You won't be,
Reality without you is hard to take,
Reality just won't be fake,

The sound of the night brings your voice to trouble me,
I gather your memories and drop a tear humbly,
How badly i wanted the moment to freeze,
When the sun shined and the air was breeze,

Pluck the flower and it will die,
I made mistakes and I did lie,
You always walked the straighter way,
I was wasted at night and played with the day,

The lander sees the ship on the horizon,
A sailor knows it's an illusion,
Pray, Let the Sun meet the Sea,
In another life, let it be, you and me.

15. Strong Dog

He said not aloud,
A secret bubble kept in his heart,
Yet seen clear in his bright eyes,
His dream,
Not the riches,
Oh no! not the gold,
But a moment,
A moment that would be His.

A moment he would fall, yet smile,
He would break, yet not hurt.

16. Small Wish

Lord, if you own everything,
And Nothing makes you less,
Make me king,
Surround me with queens,
I will thank you.

17. True

Silent Hall rooms,
Self-smiling Dinings,
Sour tamarind bed,
A prison with internet!
What more could you ask.

18. Your Masterpiece

Art takes time,
Masterpiece takes a moment.
Make your moment,
Make a Masterpiece.

19. Borders And Brackets

Borders and Boundaries and Brackets,
Are Belittling.
Forget them.

20. Not To Be

No worries,
Some Dreams are meant not to be,
Yours and Mine.

21. One Teacher

A Book gets old when it's been read often,
A Man learns when he Listens, and Speaks seldom.

22. Wish I Could Be You

The Sky unworries me with its emptiness,
Yet of Heavenly fullness,
Amazes with depth, and infinite height,
Colors defining, reflecting,
Yet nothing it has,
Nothing it owns,
And simply exists, Without existing.

23. Ecstasy

Take a deep breath,
Get high on the Evens of life,
Get kicks from the Odds of it,
Live in Ecstasy.

24. Away

In a place two times away,
Garden green n yellow,
In a bed meant for two,
You and Me, Cozy blue.

25. Intimacy

Everyone feels night and day,
Hold each other,
Sleep in each other,
Someone's day,
Someone's night.

26. She is Gone

The mind knew it all,
Heart was spellbound,
The story of the rose,
Taken away by a soft breeze,
Soothing sound,
She will Never be found!

27. Cannot Get Over

I wish God exists,

So we can get over with religion.

28. Directionless

Ignore the Landmark that is not the Moon,
We are wavy wanderers,
Let the wheel slip,
Let's lose the north,

Let the anchor rust,
Melt with me and go everywhere,
Naked on the sea and no chains,
Wild with the water and the storms.

29. Love Make

Love love love, Dear love,

Is You not that made me love,
That made me hate, little dove,

On earth, made my Heaven,
Made me sane,
That made fire Red,
Made mountain n sky wed,

That made Devil whisper,
Made God a sinner,
Made songs infinite,
Songs that soften the night,

But love, for all that is You, love,
Is not this the time to make love,

Is to say, can I say, love love, my dear love.

30. Good Bye

Till the day we meet again,
My own rain,
My own train,

Till then,
Goodbye.

31. Peace

The wars won are the ones not fought.

32. Foeticide

Unchain her from every norm,
From every worm,
Don't decide should she be out,
Of morning womb,
A law that you shake to make,
Wish you could deliver,
For the life she delivered in you,
Amazed, are you?

A seed yesterday,
She will be the rose for your tomorrow,
Just,
Justly,
Let her grow today.

33. God Heals?

Maybe you are not the one I know,
Maybe not the one I am looking for,
Not the one I thought exist?
Not the one I was made to believe?

Are you the one people call God? Ha!
Are you decorated with gold? we poor,
Are you the one with garlands of plucked flowers?
You are the one with the holy land?

Do you sleep in the clouds?
In empty skies?
Do you reside the seas?
Do I call you her or his?

I suppose you are unknown,
For the very few things known,
For the miracles you have not performed,
For the teachings untaught,

Can I ask you, would you mind?
Where are your eyes, front or hind?
Do you not see? Do you not weep?
Thousands crying, as many dying, A large heap,

I forgot to tell you,
You have the Power, you are The Truth,
All highty, all fighty, all sighty,
Don't be crazy, don't lie lazy,

Book a heart for yourself,
Read a book on trauma, and tears,
Find a mind to act, just don't be eyes to fetch,
And for things said and done, you can't hurt me if you can't heal,

I don't fear you if you are not yourself,
You are just a wind getting old,
People forget you and your norms,
Don't you worry, I won't write you off,

I dare not to carry you on a casket,
I wish you live, like lilies on a basket,
But it's late now, I've got to sleep,
I'll pray You, I'll bow you, you don't beg,

Let's make a deal,
I'll feel you, You will heal.

34. Winner

March on, March, March on,
Fear nobody, Fear nothing,
You are to win,
Nothing to lose, Everything to win,

You are the king of your dream,
You are the leader, You lead,
Crush the hill with your will,
March on, March, till you win.

35. Yet Near, Yet Far

I can tell you how I feel, but tell me,
Are you exactly what I see,
Do you mean, what you say,
Can you show what you conceal, say,

Let me ask, I'll ask every day,
Why are you not what I see,

Is it you? Where are you?
Have you painted yourself, color untrue?
Don't go so far that you can't return back,
Don't sleep so deep that you can't wake,

Don't go away. Don't.

36. Medalled And Martyred

Cry over your fate till the day ends,
Sleep with a burden on your chest,
Wake up to the numbness of the mind,
Don't fight, welcome defeat!

You are imprisoned only by the cages of your mind,
Crippled by the inability of your shivering voice,
Burying the dreams you once had, why
Killing your want, your wish, oh why

Hear! You are your greatest enemy,
The only one who can bring you down,
Discover and Defeat the rally of army fighting within,
Live to be medalled, death immortalized martyr.

37. Social Animal

You are perfectly wild for the zoo.
And domesticated, for the circus.
You are dead, suited for a box.
You can be still, A Statue,
But you will never be free.
You will Never be in the jungle.
You will never feel the beat and the thump of the rush,
You will always be The Social Animal.

38. Good Night

Can you please give me just one look from those eyes,
For I need to spend the whole night alone,
And while the night sky is filled with a million stars,
I'll be looking at the one that shines for me,
Doing nothing much, but one dream to sleep, that's it.

39. Un-Understable

I don't know if you will understand, but I get high on the sight that is your eyes,
In something so simple as my life, my complicated queen, my dear vice,

I don't know if you would understand,
I don't make sense,
Of a story of one night,
When you were in your world and my dream,
Two places at a time,
And I couldn't understand why, and how.

40. Life is Today

Life expressions,
Times we clock,
Yesterday has beautifully rivered in the memory sea,
Yesterday has died peacefully,
Will tomorrow be born, unborn,
Love, Be not sad,
Today is alive.

41. Dead Advice

The white moon is dark,
The stars are dead,
The sky is not blue,
And the wind is still, or no more,

So let me tell you,
Truth is hard to find,
Lies grow on every side,
Beware of the love that is blind,

Keep your shoes clean,
And your hands tied.

42. Unsaid

The words spoken, are not the only things said.
What you see, rest which is hidden.
The expectations, just a little higher.
Truth, hard to be told.

Hope you feel, that which I wish.

43. Sinner

The honest gave you a name, God
Faces and forms by fraud
Earth and sky is you
An unmatchable view

Tons of things learnt in school
To search for you, still a fool
To be me, as you say
All my vices, to throwaway
Said the wise man and the crook
Are your words from the good book

But rain can't wash away my deepest sin
Mirror won't change who I've seen
And in dilemma as I scream
Come to me, tonight, in my dream.

44. Time Machine

If only I had a Time Machine, I would break it, In Time.

45. In Need

Will wine taste sweet
When water is what I need
Will you be there
So much to fear

I don't remember when you bit me
Your venom just won't kill me
Will you care to love
So much more than enough

I will pull you close to my chest
Two birds in the lover's nest
Every move and every sound with a meaning, then and now,
I will dream you forever, I will vow

But when reality speaks harsh
Heart and mind wage wars
You can't get what you can't reach
Million stars and not one in your fist.

46. Tips And Tricks

School, school that taught me to walk,
But was it street, where I learned to cross,

Love, oh love! You taught me to cry,
Poor hate, with you I learned to smile,

Night, darkness, closed eyes and I could see,
Bright sunny day, I learned the art to steal,

With liars behind my back, behind bars, I lied to win,
Truth, as it fails to exist, taught me I can fail,

Life, oh life, you are amazing,
With you, I learned to be, just me.

47. Love Grows

Love grows, I guess, when we water it with constant foolishness.

48. Let me walk with you

Will you,
Let me walk this path with you,
Let me go where you,
Beside you, Behind you,
And about holding hands,
I wish to, but choose that you,
Just let me walk this path with you,
Will you.

49. For You

I can separate fact from fiction,
Stars from sky,
I can make water climb up,
Trees grow down,
Trust me when I lie,
Horses can speak to me, I can neigh,
I can make it rain,
In monsoon and any other time,
There is something I wish to tell you,
All the impossibles, just for you,

50. God is Good

God is so good,
Cared even for The Devil,
And created one in each of us!

51. Journey of the Fools-I

I told my friend,

A wise man once said,
"Be wise"
And before I could ask how?
He left.

Friend replied,

"True, I saw him too,
He went somewhere I know not, maybe north,
I was blurry eyed, narcotized,
I am eager to know him, Kno",

We went uh-north of the forest, searching,

Chilling winds, killing pricks,
Met a group of nomads, helped us with fire and food,
"Help us", we plead, "to find The Wise One",
"Join us then", One of she replied, winking at me, "Hope you are not a fool".

52. Journey of the fools-II

"I wanted to ask, should I be wised, or look for the wise one",

She lost her cool, the queen,
"Summon the one hit by the lightning bolt,
The one who survived", she ordered,
We were grateful, felt no cold, saw The Man,

I was happy and clueless, and my friend too,

"You, You told us to be wise,
We are fools, we want to be wise,
Oh learned! teach us too, please do"
He had a lisp, He recollected, and said,

"That is correct, all I said was, be nice".

53. Dreams

Flawed as a human,
We are not where our dreams are,
Let's travel to reach, for us,
A drink on the way, and no fear,

The heavens will open up for us,
The wind will be un-still,
The night will wait,
And when we look up, The rain will bless on us,

And love, All dreams will come true,
Won't it.

54. Beautiful blue lit aquarium

Beautiful blue lit aquarium, Freedom, For Fishes,

Food, Well-made bed, Prison, For people,

Marketing jingles, Study tours, Zoos, Lovely Animals,

Books, Tests, Pressured peers, Fails, Blessed Schools,

Age, green hedge, War, Killer, Proud Badge,

Heavy heart, un-souled, mind dense, Sage,

Salvation, Serenity, Peaced bliss, Non-Sense.

55. Memoir

I saw her, first time, on the eastern side of the river,
It was a cold night, and I was sweating with fever,

She came with a drape and a leafy pillow,
Her hands were comforting, and face was sunny yellow,

Words describing love came to me but I carried a spear, half naked, and I had to go,
She watched me swim river and her eyes were swimming so,

On the western side was a game of blood n lies, rage,
Gold and Kings and Queens, and I had orders, and I won, I was not a sage,

And finite life, infinite wars, and weakening shoes and sight,
I had a broken spear, unsent letters I would write,

And the bridge I could not cross, and the pigeon I could not find,
But I had to gather lost courage, I would not survive, she not with me but in mind,

The east was still pure, and I was feeling a beating heart,
I prepared lots of lies and excuses, also, I planned a wedding kart,

I reached her abode, people in plenty, Welcoming me maybe,
My healing chest, was again wound pierced, I was knee down, blurry, snaky, shaky,

I joined to carry her to her grotto, and I could not see the rainbow,
Her daughter told me, she knew I would always come, today or tomorrow,

Today, my heart will beat again, I will visit her, I prayed heaven to God, I am in my casket,
I goodbyed happy to friends, kept flowers, flowers for her, in a yellow basket.

56. Far From Love

Lord, let it not be love that grips me,
The lover makes me see faces,
Of everybody, holding blood-red-white roses,
Cold winter comes crawling like the serpent,
Whips like steel,
And people are gone, friends and foe, family,
Love, scar, wanting, haunting, breaking,
And the bed that has wicked thorns,
Feeling of sliced cut spine, empty,

I pray let it not be love that gets me,
The cries bleeding, from piercing chest,
Maybe death can give me rest,
Horrified, into sunken skulls with dead eyes,
Poison on my palm,
Screaming, and peeling my skin,
Gives me no calm,
Give me a drop of water, scratched throat, give it with gin,
I cannot take love that gets,

Am I so far away from love,
Tell me, love,
Am I far from love.

57. In Peace

The time machine can take me back to the done days,
And I will fix all the things broken,
Do everything the right way,
A clean slate, if only a time machine.

But, is it satisfying, the truth, realization,
There are always regrets in life,
There are always the good times to cherish,
And a desire that will always remain.

58. She

The sight of she, so mystically beautiful,
The body of Egyptian grace,
Lips of torturous want,
Black eyes of red opium,
The longing and the seeking,
Evil desire that grows for her,
The desires.

She is the goddess that steps on the heart and clouds my mind.

59. #MeToo

Pride, not to be kept above the head,
Nor under the shoe, say not for me,
But on the chest, wear it like a badge,
Tell them loud, I am me too,

60. Break Free

Walking down the asphalt, collecting dust
Alone in a bunch, who to trust
trouble-ride, will it end
angel with answer, who would send

Questions troubling your night,
Be brave, soon says light,
seek beyond your darkest fear
call out when you hear

There is a door that is waiting to open
There is, give up being broken
live and smile to the mirror
Today, let your will, your wings, be seen clearer.

61. NightSky Love

The color of the night made pleasant,
By a distant moon and 26 stars,
Listen to your own breath and gaze,
The way of the sky is to amaze,
Paint the sky with your thought, uncomprehend,
Create a secret with your name,
The drift into the maze can take you home,
The puzzle that everyone loves to solve,
The vastness that is unconquered,
The calmness unrippled,
The sound that is silent.

62. Lets Breathe

The dying sun will rise again if we promise love,
And the moon with the spots will cover us for a night of peace, and pleasure,
The tree with a thousand leaves will let us sit, and we can ponder,
The run of the river will make music for our saddened hearts to feel,
The mountains will bow down for us to conquer, One day.

With a good god, all we need is to breathe.

63. Hospitalization

Aliens, I saw them, last night,
Not in the skies,
Somewhere, blurry, bright light,
They thrashed me to my bed,
Big ears, big eyes, minors' age,
Two spoke something mandarin, One was from the west,
Travelled far and wide to disrupt me sleep,
Talked with me for four hours,
I couldn't understand language or reason, just gestures,
Later, one other came, He said, And I could understand,
"You are drunk, you need stitches,
We are friends from your own galaxy",

In a dramatic end, they pointed at me, and waved goodbye,
"You are Hospitalized".

64. I Am A Rock

I am a rock figurine, I roll alone,
Stranger to feel, hell in heel,

As hard as I may be, You, I feel,
So let's have a deal,
If the time comes to go down, If,
Let's roll together, till river is reached,

In a boat above the waters, will take,
Through woods, through sights, sightseeing,
Luck may be good, and we may reach by dusk,
To the shores, And We can chase our own sun.

65. Meditation

Meditation, a cure for some, relief for most,
Let me teach you,
Sit on a mattress, if you don't find grass,
Crossed legs,
Close your eyes, and no grin on the chin,
Close your ears and see no traffic, trucks,
Breathing is important, But you may choose not to,
Different procedure altogether,
We will discuss it later,
Let your mind float in the direction sun is good,
Or moon is great, or somewhere else,
Let your hands free,
Show fingers three,
Remember names and smile,
All your memories worthwhile,
Meditate your life.

66. Love In A Bank

Times ago, I opened an account with you,
You remember? I vaguely do,

I can't afford another me,
Expensively lived in a rented paradise,

Years and years of shiny rum n ride,
And there, there is insolvency by my side,

Must sell myself to you,
Clear all my dues, settlements, I owe you,

Current and savings, you,
Loans and bygones, you,

Interest wise, forgive me, I love you.

67. The Week

In a world where every day is Sunday, I

Would be happy, very happy,
Existing in holidays, absent dry days,

I would also be sad kno, very sad,
For the Mondays, and the fri-cry-days,

But,
Let's be ok with the weekdays, and the weekends,
Eat with family, Drink with friends,
And the sentiments.

68. To You

The extra blanket,
Me and you,

The extra pen,
Pages for you,

The extra me,
I am in you,

The one heart,
For you,
Just you.

69. Equality

In my vision of an equal world,

I want to be blinded from
The sinner and the saint,
The house and the hut,
The pauper and the prince,

Just want my ten from the twenty,
The poem from the poetry.

70. Love Night

All lights have been dimmed,
Both have their eyes winked,
Candle one and two lit,
Day is suspended, let's meet.

71. Conqueror

Oceans and mountains, when the time comes, shall be conquered.

72. Stuck Tear

I need that tear,
That is stuck inside flipping,
One tear,
That can,
Heave-Ho!! Lighten the heart and the night,
And amaze me with child joy.

73. Lost A Friend

But I can cry,
I refuse to show, or shed any tear,
I feel my eyes swell,
And heart fear,

But I will crunch a fist,
Lacerate my skin,
Grind my teeth,
I will commit any sin,

I will fight all the gods,
Tell them their faults,
Haunt them like ghosts,
Just I am not to break, I feel,

So, for now, Let me float my heart,
I will ease myself, RIP, My Friend.

Thank You

www.ingramcontent.com/pod-product-compliance
Ingram Content Group UK Ltd.
Pitfield, Milton Keynes, MK11 3LW, UK
UKHW041844200726
13854UKWH00005BA/2067

9 798888 695197